Amazing Experiments with
Electricity
and Magnetism

Text: Paula Navarro & Àngels Jiménez
Illustrations: Bernadette Cuxart

BARRON'S

Contents

The simplest motor in the world, 4

The magnetic shark, 6

The citrus connection, 8

The magic balloon, 10

The pirate compass, 12

A homemade speaker, 14

Let's make an electromagnet, 16

Conductor or non-conductor? That is the question, 18

Glasses that give off sparks, 20

The spinning cake mold, 22

A can race, 24

A pendulum with personality, 26

The compass goes crazy!, 28

The swinging grapes, 30

This pencil is electrifying me!, 32

Without coverage!, 34

Objectives of this book

Here you have the fourth and final book in the "Magic Science" series. In *Amazing Experiments with Electricity and Magnetism*, we take matters even further with the most complex scientific topics, but in a fun and simple manner so that boys and girls between 6 and 12 years old can conduct the experiments confidently.

The book handles a scientific topic that has not been greatly disseminated or tested, that of electricity and magnetism. Thanks to this book, the boys and girls will be able to understand what electricity is, what types of electricity there are, which materials are conductors and which ones are insulators of electricity, what magnetic fields are and how they behave, as well as other concepts that are directly related to objects you can find at home, because today we live in a world that depends on electricity.

Unlike the three previous volumes, *Amazing Experiments with Electricity and Magnetism* contains experiments that require the supervision of an adult or an older child and that require that several children work together, because this book contains the most complex experiments of the four volumes in the series, as the culmination of them all. Thus, the participation of several generations is encouraged, enabling an educational and fun experience to be shared.

Let the boys and girls become "electrified" with this entralling book!

The simplest motor in the world

You will need:
- Scissors
- A disc-shaped magnet
- A 1.5 V (AA) battery
- A reel of copper wire

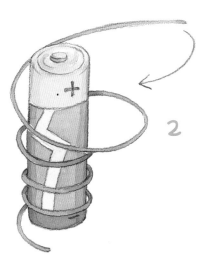

1 Cut a length of copper wire equal to about the width of your widespread hands, roughly 8 inches. Cut it firmly, as it's a bit hard. There!

2 Roll the piece of copper around the battery, forming a spiral. It will end up like a hair ringlet! How artistic; it looks like a modern art sculpture!

3 Bend one end of the copper wire toward the positive end of the battery (you know, it has a + sign). Without changing the shape of the copper, open the spiral slightly so that the copper will be able to turn... in other words, make it a bit larger.

4 Set the spiral aside and now place the magnet on the negative end of the battery (the end with the – sign). You will see that it sticks there. Click!

5 Now place the spiral of copper wire around the battery and connect both terminals, one tip on the positive pole and the other on the negative pole, but touching the side of the magnet.

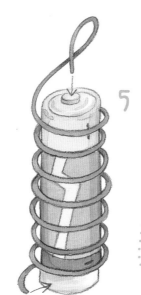

Why does it happen?

An **electric motor is a machine that transforms electrical energy into mechanical energy**, that is, into movement. In this experiment, you have just built the simplest possible electric motor! When the copper wire touches the magnet, you close the circuit and an electrical current passes through it. Given that it is found inside a magnetic field (which is what the magnet produces), a force is generated that makes the wire spin around the magnet. Thus, you have converted the electric energy provided by the battery into mechanical energy, which makes the copper wire move and spin!

6 Try it out!
Place the battery standing up on a table with the copper wire connected. You will see that it starts to spin endlessly! Wow! What a fun scientific dizzy spell!

The magnetic shark

1 The first step implies going into artistic mode and drawing 3 or 4 figures on the paper. We've drawn a shark and some fish, so that the end effect will be more fun. Then give your shark a blue- gray color and paint the fish in bright colors.

1

You will need:
- Cardboard
- Sheets of paper
- Scissors
- Glue
- Double-sided tape
- Colored pencils
- Paper clips
- A ruler
- Thick string
- A small magnet

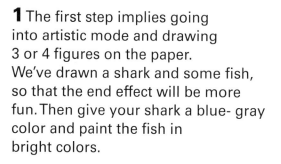

2 Cut the figures out using the scissors, being careful to go over the pencil outline.

3 Glue the shark onto the piece of cardboard. Then cut around the outline so you will have a much stronger and more resistant shark!

4 Place a piece of double-sided tape on one side of the magnet and stick it onto the shark in the middle of the cardboard side. Don't make a mistake, the shark won't be able to catch the fish!

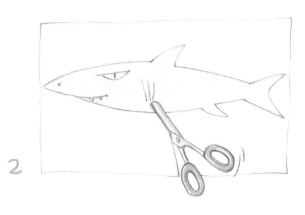

2

3

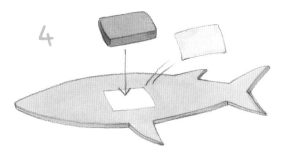

4

Why does it happen?

Although they seem magical, **magnets are simply natural stones that were discovered thousands of years ago**, like magnetite and calamite. There are also artificial magnets that are made by blending metals. And why do they attract iron? Well, because of the fact that objects are made up of atoms, which have small electrical charges. You need to imagine that there are many tiny magnets inside them. Normally, they are all mixed up and don't produce any effects, but in the case of magnets, they are well ordered and act like a single magnet. That's why they can attract or repel iron (and some other metals).

5 Cut a length of string, a couple of palms long. Tie one end to the ruler and the other end around the magnet, strengthening it with a little glue. It will end up like a fishing rod. Now it's time to prepare the food for the shark, which will be the little colorful fish, each with a paper clip.

6 Try it out!
Place the fish on the floor or on a table and then... Yum, yum... The shark notices these delicious fish... The poor thing is very hungry... He approaches them and... Crunch! He catches them one by one!

The citrus connection

1 Hold the lemons at both ends and stick one of the copper pennies into it; stick the coin in firmly about halfway.

2 In the same upper half of the lemon where you stuck the coin, stick the screw, but on the opposite side, that is, one in front of the other. Oh, the poor lemon!

You will need:
- A couple of lemons
- Two galvanized zinc screws
- Two copper pennies
- Scissors
- Conductor cables (copper)
- A low-intensity LED (we use 2V)

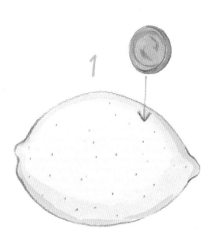

3 With the help of the scissors, very carefully strip the end of the wire, removing its plastic cover. It would be better to ask an adult or an older brother or sister to help you, because it's quite a complicated step. Do the same thing with the other wire, to make two. That's it, well stripped!

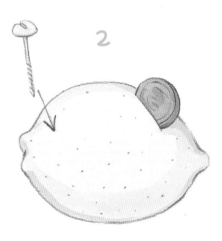

4 Connect a cable to the screw, rolling the stripped end of the cable around it. Connect the other cable to the coin; it's best to make a U-shape and check that it stays well attached to the coin.

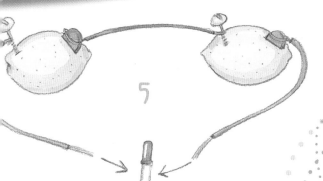

5 Now take the other lemon and stick the corresponding coin and screw into it. Connect the end of the wire from the first screw to the coin in the second lemon and the coin in the first lemon to the screw in the second one. Cut this last wire in half and strip the ends as shown in the drawing: You're going to connect it to an LED.

Why does it happen?

You connected two **different metals** to these "guinea pig" lemons: **a galvanized screw made of zinc and a coin made of copper, which forms electrodes.** Zinc is a metal that gives electrons (the anode), and copper on the other hand receives them (the cathode). At the other end, the lemon juice enables the electrons to pass from one metal to the other, creating a very small electrical current. Both lemons must be connected for the LED to work. You would need more than 5,000 lemons to light up a lightbulb in one of the lamps in the house, but that would be impossible! You can try doing the same thing with different fruit and vegetables: potatoes, apples, etc.

6 Try it out!

Lastly, connect the end of each cable to the LED rods. You cannot connect it any other way, because the LED only works in one way! So, the largest rod of the LED goes with the cable attached to the coin and the short rod goes with the cable attached to the screw. You'll see that as soon as you connect them the LED lights up! Wow! But to see it better, you can switch off the lights.

The magic balloon

1 First you need to demonstrate your lung capacity. Blow up the balloon until it's quite large (but don't wait for it to burst!) and tie a knot in the end.

You will need:
- A large container (to hold an inflated balloon)
- Water
- A woolen scarf
- Confetti
- A light-colored balloon
- A felt-tipped pen

2 Decorate the balloon as you like. Smiley faces are very cool, and we're not going to play any tricks on this balloon.

3 Place the confetti in the container. You don't need to fill it up, as it would overflow and then it would be difficult to tidy up. You only need a little to appreciate the effect!

4 Rub the happy balloon's head with the woolen scarf. It looks like you're polishing his bald head!

5 Place the balloon near the container... and you will see that the confetti sticks to it! He has suddenly grown some hair! Look how handsome he is!

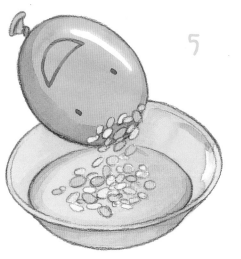

6 Try it out!

You can also try doing the same thing, but instead of sticking confetti on him, you will make a stream of water change course. You can do so with water from the tap or a jug of water.

Why does it happen?

Sometimes, when you rub two objects together, such as the wool and the balloon, one of them can give electrons to the other. So the balloon takes the electrons that the wool gives it, and this means that it becomes negatively charged. That's why, when you place the balloon near the confetti, it attracts the positive charges and it all sticks to the balloon, resulting in an improvised multi-colored wig! In this very simple way, **you have generated static electricity!**

The pirate compass

1 Pour water into the container to a height of about 2 fingers' width, enough for the compass boat you are going to make to float in.

You will need:
◆ Aluminum foil
◆ Water
◆ A large container to pour the water in
◆ A magnet
◆ A sewing needle
◆ Felt-tipped pen
◆ Scissors
◆ Tape
◆ Paper
◆ Glue
◆ A drinking straw

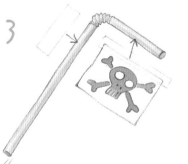

2 Cut a piece of aluminum foil. The size should be roughly like your outstretched hand. Give this square or rectangular-shaped piece of aluminum the shape of a boat by raising the edges.

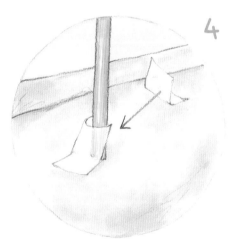

3 Decorate the boat as you wish. We used a straw and a piece of paper to make a pirate flag! Use tape to join the flag to the mast.

4 Then stick the mast onto the boat. It doesn't need to be heavy, otherwise the boat would sink and the experiment wouldn't work well.

5 Carefully hold the needle in the middle and rub it with a magnet for a while. That's it! With the strength of a pirate, very good!

Why does it happen?

Our planet is like a gigantic magnet; it has **magnetism that forms in its nucleus.** When you rub the needle with the magnet, you magnetize it. In other words, you convert it into a small magnet with its north pole and its south pole, just like the Earth. So, **in the same way that two magnets are attracted to one another by opposite poles and repel one another at the equal poles, the needle, which is now a small magnet, is attracted by the Earth.** That's why you see that the boat moves when you place the needle in it: It points north, just like a compass!

6 Try it out!

When you have rubbed it well, place the needle inside the boat, in the middle. Wait for the water to settle down, and gradually you will see that this wonderful pirate compass points north!

A homemade speaker

1 The first step consists of making a coil with the copper wire, turning it into an O shape. For it to work, you need to roll a length of copper wire about 5 feet long. Close the two ends jutting out from the coil by passing them behind it, as shown in the drawing.

2 Take the speaker wire and separate the two cables slightly by pulling at them with your hands. Then strip the tips a little with some scissors (with the help of an adult) to make the connection with the coil.

You will need:
- A device for playing music
- 1 or 2 mm thick copper wire
- Speaker wire
- A magnet
- Scissors
- Insulating tape
- Different types of cups (plastic, paper, large, and small)

3 Connect each end of the cables you have stripped to each end of the wire coil. Do so by twisting them together, like a braid or a spiral. Make sure that they are well attached, joined together forever!

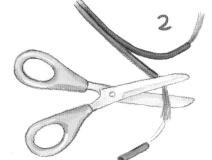

4 Cover the joins with a little insulating tape. It's easy: Wrap the tape around, attach it well, and cut off the overlapping piece.

5 You also have to separate the other end of the speaker wire and also strip both ends... Now you have to connect them to the music player. Normally at the back music players have little inlets where the cables emitting the music are placed.

Why does it happen?

What happens in this experiment is that **two magnetic fields collide: The one that the natural magnet has collides with the one produced by the copper coil when the electrical current** passes along its wire. A force is generated and this makes the coil shake crazily on top of the magnet, in time with the music. The little jumps of the coil mean that the sound is conveyed, because sound is precisely the vibration you detect. The cup works as an amplifier so you can hear the music much better! Dance, thanks to the homemade speaker!

6 Try it out!

Turn on the music player, place the magnet near it and the coil on the magnet. Why? Well, to listen to the music! If you place different sized cups on the coil, you will notice that you can hear (not very loudly) the sound of the song being played on the music player! Ooh! Now you don't need such bulky speakers!

Let's make an electromagnet

You will need:
- ◆ A 9V battery
- ◆ A spoon
- ◆ Conductor cable
- ◆ Paper clips
- ◆ Plasticine
- ◆ A tool for cutting Plasticine

1 Cut a small piece of Plasticine to serve as a base to place the battery. A piece the width of 2 or 3 fingers will be enough. It works very well because it holds the battery perfectly, and it's a clean system that is easy to model!

2 Fix the battery to the Plasticine well. To do so, sink the bottom of the battery into the middle of the Plasticine... but just a little! With the leftover piece of Plasticine, make a kind of "L" to make the lid over the top of the battery. You have to be careful with all the details, okay?

3 Now take the spoon and the conductor cable with the two ends stripped and roll the cable around the handle of the spoon. But don't roll it around entirely! The two ends must stick out, as if the spoon had two antennae!

1

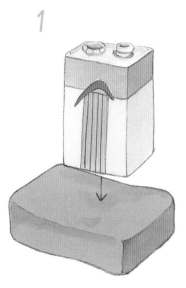

2

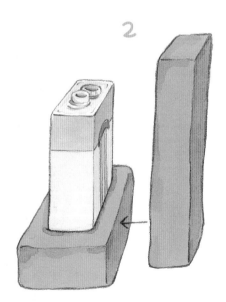

3

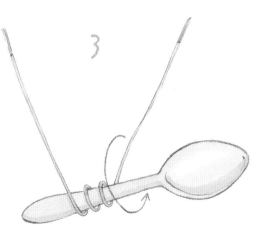

4

4 Connect the two ends of the cable to the poles of the battery (the two little bumps at the top of the battery).

5 Lastly, close the top with another piece of Plasticine, so that the cables cannot come loose.

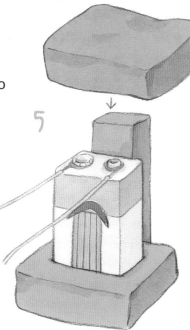

Why does it happen?

When you roll the cable around the spoon, you make a coil through which you make the electrical current circulate when you connect the two ends of the cable to the battery. The movement of electrons through the coil also generates a magnetic field, which magnetizes the spoon that is positioned right in the middle of the coil. So, **it magnetizes it, converting it into a magnet!** Now, the spoon is capable of attracting small metallic objects! Be careful not to try attracting large objects, because the attraction force of the spoon is very limited!

6 Try it out!

And finally, for the spectacular step: Bring the end of the spoon close to a paper clip and pick it up! It looks like spoon magic, but it's an electromagnet you've made yourself! You can even make a chain of paper clips!

Conductor or non-conductor? That is the question

You will need:
- ◆ 3 small glasses
- ◆ Water
- ◆ Oil
- ◆ Alcohol
- ◆ A 9V battery
- ◆ Plasticine
- ◆ Scissors
- ◆ A 2V LED
- ◆ 2 conductor cables
- ◆ Tissue paper
- ◆ A piece of black construction paper

1 Strip the ends of the cables with the scissors. Do so for both cables and on both ends of the cables.

2 Roll the ends of the two cables around the poles of the battery. To secure them, place a little Plasticine on top, now that you've seen that this works very well.

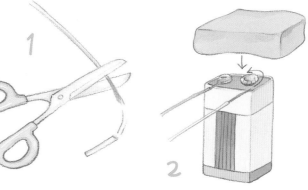

3 Roll the other ends of the stripped cables around the rods of the LED. Check that it works and that the LED lights up, as the LED connections only work in one direction. If you look carefully, you'll see that one rod is longer than the other and this is to distinguish between the positive pole (the long rod) and the negative pole (the short rod). Now cut one of the cables in half and strip the ends, as you see in the image. Then support the LED with a little Plasticine and place a piece of black card behind it, so that you can see whether it lights up well or not.

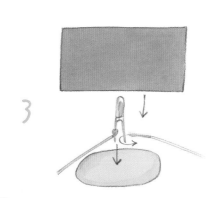

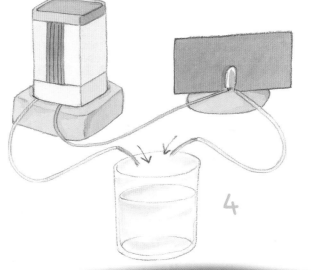

4 Pour some water into one of the glasses. Place the two newly stripped free cable ends into the water, one that leads to the battery and the other the LED. What happens to the LED?

To check that it isn't a trick, remove the cables from the water and you will see that the LED does not light up!

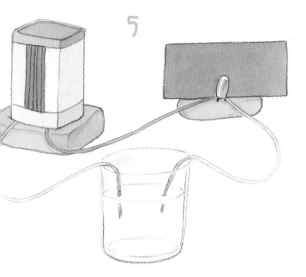

5 Now test it with oil. Pour a little oil into the other glass and try placing the cables inside (clean the tips first). Does it light up?

Why does it happen?

Some **liquids are conductors of electricity** and others are not. Mineral water has a lot of dissolved minerals, which makes it a good conductor of electricity; the electrons can circulate freely and the LED lights up. On the other hand, with oil you saw that the LED did not light up, because unlike water it is an insulator and does not conduct electricity. Alcohol is a slightly better conductor of electricity than oil, but not as good as water, and you saw that the LED lit up but not as strongly as with water. That's why they tell you that it is very dangerous to place any electrical appliance near water!

6 Try it out!

Conduct a final test with alcohol! You will see that the LED lights up, but slightly less than with water. Now you have seen which liquids are good conductors of electricity and which ones are not! Take note!

19

Glasses that give off sparks

1 Cut out three rectangles of aluminum foil. They must be large enough to wrap around the plastic cups.

You will **need:**
- Aluminum foil
- Scissors
- Two plastic cups
- 2V LED
- A balloon
- A woolen scarf

2 Now cover the two cups with the aluminum foil. Leave a slight margin, without covering the top part, as shown in the drawing. It's best to cover the cups by rolling them.

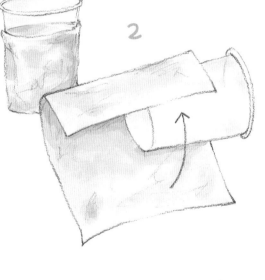

3 With the other piece of aluminum foil that you have cut out, fold a short, thin rectangle and place it in one of the cups, between the aluminum foil and the plastic cup. It looks like it's sticking its tongue out at you, doesn't it?

4 Place the cup with the rectangle inside the other cup, just like when you tidy them up and stack them one inside the other.

5 Blow up the balloon and rub it with the scarf so that it becomes charged with static electricity, then bring it near the tip of the aluminum foil jutting out from the cup. Do so 5 or 6 times.

Why does it happen?

In this experiment, **you have made a** very simple **condenser. The two cups with aluminum foil store the charges received by the balloon that you rubbed** with the wool. It works like a small cupboard in which you store things, in this case, electrical charges! When you hold the outer cup with one hand touching the metallic part and bring a finger from the other hand toward the piece of aluminum foil, you create a path through yourself by which all those stored charges can emerge from the condenser. That's why you feel a small shock! Ouch!

6 Try it out!
With the tip of your finger, bravely touch the aluminum foil that you have charged with electricity using the balloon, and with the other hand hold the aluminum foil that is covering the other cup, so as to close the circuit. Ouch! What was that? A little spark jumped from the cup to your finger!

The spinning cake mold

1 Fill the container almost to the brim with water—almost, because you know that water is a scarce resource! You can also reuse it afterward to water the plants!

1

You will need:
- A large container such as a bowl
- A jug of water
- A cake mold
- Colored stickers
- Tape
- A long wooden stick
- A neodymium magnet

2

2 Decorate the cake mold with the colored stickers to make it look nice and also to better see the spinning effect that you will obtain at the end of the experiment.

3 Stick the neodymium magnet onto the tip of the wooden stick with a little tape.

3

4

4 Place the cake mold on the water in the middle of the container and wait for the water to become very calm!

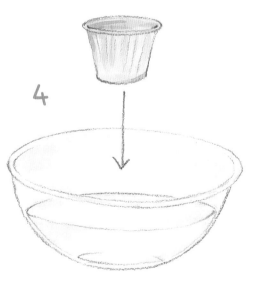

22

5 Place the stick with the magnet in the center of the cake mold and turn it to the right, tracing small circles. What does the cake mold do? It follows you, as if it were hypnotized! It's as if you had a magic wand!

5

Why does it happen?

Cake molds are not magnets and they are not attracted by them. You can check this easily if you bring one close to a magnet: You won't notice any effect, because it is not magnetic. But on the other hand, aluminum is a conductor of electricity! When you move the magnet in circles near the cake mold, you cause a movement of charges to form inside some currents, called **Eddy Currents**, which are magnetic fields that make the cake mold move as if it were hypnotized by the magnet!

6

6 Try it out!
Now make the stick turn in the opposite direction, to the left, also tracing circles. The cake mold does the same! Ooh! This spinning cake mold must be getting very dizzy!

A can race

You will need:
- Two drinks cans
- Different-colored tape
- Scissors
- A felt-tipped pen
- Two different-colored balloons
- A scarf or piece of wool

1

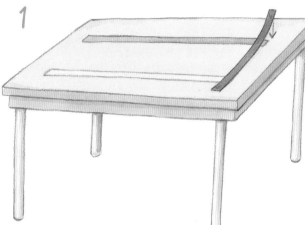

1 Take two different-colored tapes and stick about 30 cm lengths of them on a surface where they can be seen well. These strips will be the lanes where the race will be held. Mark the finish line well too, of course!

2

2 Decorate the bottoms of the cans a little by drawing a motif or placing a sticker, such as the logos of two rival sports clubs!

3 Place each can at the starting line and line them up well—without cheating!

3

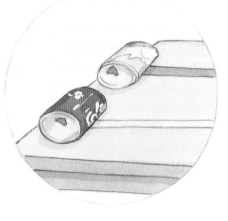

4

4 Blow up the balloon and tie the end. Then do the same with the other colored balloon. You could ask a friend to blow too and place bets on which can will win!

5

Why does it happen?

Here we have another case of static electricity in which the victory will go to the player who manages to transfer the most number of electrons to the balloon. When you rub the balloons with the wool, the wool charges it, as it passes the charge to the balloon. The cans are made of aluminum and are normally at rest, that is, they have the same number of positive charges as negative ones. **When you approach it with the balloon, which is negatively charged, it attracts the positive charges in the can.** As a result, the can is attracted by the balloon and follows it, as if it were hypnotized!

5 Rub both balloons with a scarf or piece of wool, as this is ideal for charging them with static electricity. Rub, rub, rub...

6

6 Try it out!
Bring each balloon close to its can, but without touching it, and... you will see that the cans move toward the finish line! See who is the fastest, you or your friend!

A pendulum with personality

You will need:
- Lentils or rice
- A medium-sized container with a lid
- String
- A piece of cardboard
- Tape
- A pencil
- Scissors
- A hammer
- A magnet

1 Fill the container with the lentils or rice and close it. The objective is for it to be heavy, not to make a delicious dish! Fill it halfway, but you can add more weight later if you realize that it isn't enough.

2 Stick the pencil to the lid with a little tape. It should be well fixed so that it cannot come off!

3 Take the string and tie it to the magnet, going around it and tying a knot. To secure it better, you can place a little tape on the magnet.

4 Finish assembling your pendulum. How? Well, cut the string so that the magnet is one finger's width distance from the hammer underneath, leaving enough length to tie the string to the pencil. And then tie the string to the pencil.

Why does it happen?

When you make the pendulum move over the cardboard, the pendulum follows its own movement, because the cardboard is not attracted by the magnet; it does not exert any effect on it. In this case, the pendulum would end up stopping when the air that surrounds it slows it down. On the other hand, **when you place the hammer underneath, the magnet, with its magnetic field, has an attractive effect on the hammer, which slows it down** gradually, every time it passes over it. You will see that it is deflected until it eventually stops!

5 Place the cardboard underneath the magnet and swing the pendulum that you have made. Check what kind of movement it has: the typical pendulum movement, right?

6 Try it out!

Now place the hammer underneath the magnet as you did before. Release the magnet from one side and observe how it swings... Or maybe not?!

The compass goes crazy!

You will need:
- ◆ A compass
- ◆ Different electrical appliances (hair dryer, blender, etc.)

1 First, check that your compass works correctly. Otherwise, you're off to a bad start...

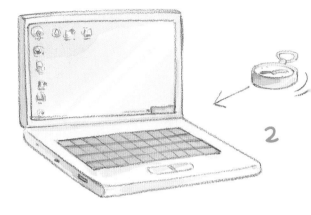

2 First choose an electrical appliance that doesn't need to be plugged in to work, that has a battery... such as a portable computer! Move the compass toward it and... what happens? It's changed position!

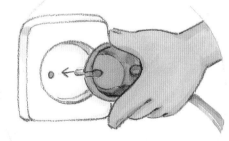

3 Maybe it's something to do with the computer... Try it out with an appliance that needs to be plugged in, like a hair dryer! Plug it in and switch it on. Don't put your fingers in!

4 Bring the compass very slowly to the hair dryer... Does it also move?

5 Make another test with a device at hand, such as the music player in the bedroom! Maybe the music will settle the compass down. First try holding it far away and then move it slowly toward the device and… well, well, the same thing happens!

Why does it happen?

In this experiment, you have just demonstrated that **electrical currents,** the movement of electrical charges, **form magnetic fields around them.** When you move the compass close to the electrical devices, it is deflected because it detects the effects of the magnetic field that are formed by the electrical device when you plug it in. The effect is more noticeable with electrical devices that have motors, such as the hair dryer, the mixer, and the fan. Try it out!

6 Try it out!

Now, out of curiosity, and to finish confirming that the compass doesn't like electrical devices… or that they make it a little nervous… try bringing it close to other devices you have at home, like a blender, a toaster, a radio, or an electric razor. Do you see what happens?

The swinging grapes

You will need:
- Two containers of equal height with large openings
- A ruler
- Tape
- Scissors
- String
- A wooden toothpick
- A straw
- A neodymium magnet
- Two grapes

1 Place the two containers some distance apart so that they can support the ruler. Place the ruler on them and secure it to the containers with tape.

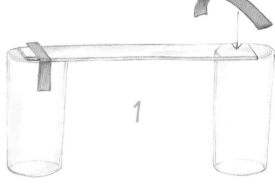

2 Tie one end of the string to the middle of the ruler and tighten it until it hangs and almost touches the surface (leave a margin of about 4 fingers' width) and cut the string. Snip!

3 Tie the wooden toothpick to the end of the string you have just cut. Tie it in the middle of the toothpick using a very strong knot! A double knot is best!

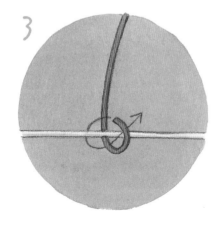

4 Choose two grapes that are about the same size and stick one onto each end of the toothpick so that they are well balanced. Very good! The toothpick should be very straight!

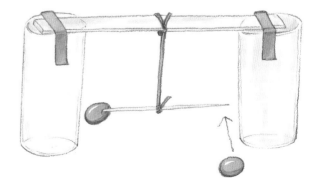

30

5 Make a kind of magic wand with the neodymium magnet, the straw, and the tape. How? Just stick the magnet on the end of the straw.

Why does it happen?

How is it possible that a grape, which is a fruit, repels the magnet? The secret is that the grape, like many other fruits, is made of water, and **water is a diamagnetic substance.** Exactly the opposite of the iron, which is attracted to the magnet, water, just like gold, graphite, and bronze, is repelled by the magnet. The grape is not rebellious and trying to escape from the magnet discretely, but rather this phenomenon of diamagnetism is very weak.

6 Try it out!

Now you simply have to bring the magnet near the grapes. But just go near them—don't touch them! You will see that the swing moves away from the magnet! Ooh! So what are the grapes made of then?

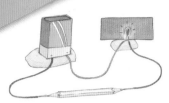

This pencil is electrifying me!

1 The first step is one that you have already done before and it worked well. Otherwise, ask an adult to help you. It's time to strip the conductor cables!

You will need:
- Conductor cables
- Scissors
- Plasticine
- A 9V battery
- A 2V LED
- A pencil
- A pencil sharpener
- A sheet of paper
- A piece of black construction paper

2 And what are you going to do with these stripped cables? Well, take each cable and connect it to the 9V battery. And to stop them from moving, you can secure them with a piece of fantastic Plasticine.

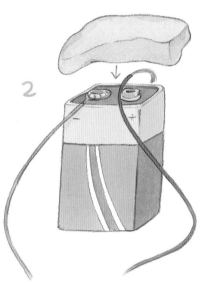

3 Roll the other ends of the cables around the ends of the LED rods. Remember that the LED only works when they are connected in one direction. If you look carefully, one end of the LED is longer than the other: It serves to distinguish the positive pole from the negative pole. To then check whether the LED lights up, place a piece of black construction paper behind the LED and secure it with a piece of Plasticine.

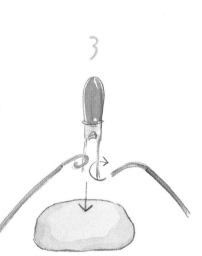

4 Now take the pencil and sharpen it well! Don't just sharpen one tip, do so at both ends so that you have two tips. Great for drawing, isn't it?

5 Cut one of the wires in half and strip the ends, which you will use to "connect" the pencil.

6 Try it out!

Check that the LED lights up when you put it in contact with the tips (that is, the ends of the cables with the tips of the pencils) and goes out when you separate the ends or when you touch the wooden part of the pencil with them. We already told you that the pencil was really great! It's electrifying!

Why does it happen?

Not only are some liquids conductors of electricity, but, as we have seen in this experiment, there are also **solids** that are **conductors** and others that are insulators. **The graphite of the pencil transmits the electrical charges** and that's why you can use it to improvise this electrical circuit and light up the LED. It doesn't work with the wood of the pencil, because it is an insulator and doesn't allow the electricity to pass through, just like the plastic covering the cables. So you can touch them without getting electrocuted!

Without coverage!

You will need:
- Aluminum foil
- Scissors
- An alarm clock
- Two cell phones

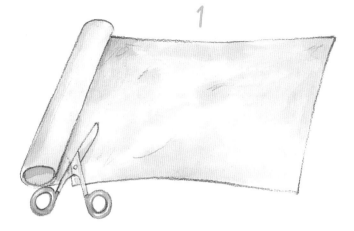

1 Unroll a little aluminum foil—just a little—and cut off a piece about tabloid size (11 x 17 inches).

2 Fold it in half and then fold the sides very well. It won't do for sending a letter, but it will be fine for this experiment!

3 Take your alarm clock from the bedside table and activate the alarm so that it starts going off. What a racket! It's like when you have to get up in the morning, isn't it?

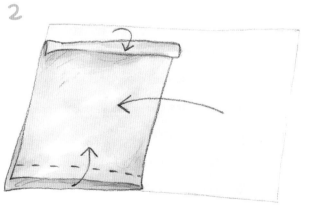

4 Place the alarm clock inside the aluminum envelope, close it well, and you'll notice that it keeps going off, even though it is inside.

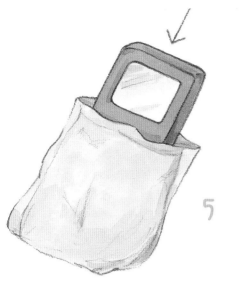

5 Remove the annoying alarm clock from the envelope and now place one of the cell phones inside and close the envelope again. You don't need to use tape; it works just by folding it.

Why does it happen?

When you wrap the alarm clock in the aluminum foil, you continue hearing the alarm, because despite being enclosed in an aluminum cage, the sound can pass through. But the same thing doesn't happen with the electromagnetic waves used by telecommunications. **Cell phones and radios, etc., work by capturing waves, and they cannot pass through metallic cages like the one you've just built.** This device is called a **Faraday Cage** and it is used a lot in aviation to protect electronic devices.

6 Try it out!

With the other cell phone, call the number of the phone that is "enclosed" inside the aluminum foil bag... and... does it ring? But it was working a moment ago! Wow, you get a message that the phone is switched off or without coverage! How is this possible?

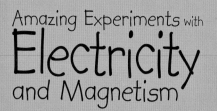

Amazing Experiments with
Electricity
and Magnetism

First edition for the United States and Canada published in 2014 by Barron's Educational Series, Inc.

Copyright © Gemser Publications, S.L. 2014
C/ Castell, 38; Teià (08329) Barcelona, Spain (World Rights)
Tel: 93 540 13 53
E-mail: info@mercedesros.com
Website: mercedesros.com

Text: Paula Navarro & Àngels Jiménez

Illustrations: Bernadette Cuxart

Design and layout: Estudi Guasch, S.L.

All inquiries should be addressed to:
Barron's Educational Series, Inc.
250 Wireless Boulevard
Hauppauge, New York 11788
www.barronseduc.com

ISBN: 978-1-4380-0428-0

Library of Congress Control
    Number: 2013943486

Date of Manufacture: May 2014
Place of Manufacture: L. REX PRINTING
    COMPANY LIMITED, Dongguan City,
    Guangdong, China

Printed in China
9 8 7 6 5 4 3 2 1